Manipulative Eye Contact Techniques:

Install thoughts and feelings just with your eyes!

Jack N. Raven

No part of this book may be reproduced or transmitted in any form whatsoever, electronic, or mechanical, including photocopying, recording, or by any informational storage or retrieval system without express permission from the author.

Copyright © 2014 Jack N. Raven Publishing Company

All rights reserved.

ISBN-13:
978-1495254062

ISBN-10:
1495254062

Table of Contents

Introduction 4

Specifics 5

Duration of Gaze 6

Strong eye contact 6

Eye contact in job hunting 7

Rewards and Punishments through the eyes 8

   Rewarding 8

   Punishments 9

Indicators of Interest 10

How to show fascination with the eyes 12

Eye communications for instant isolation 13

Making subtexts real 14

The Intimidation Look 16

Forcing submission in a Seduction setting 17

Mission Impossible Seductions 19

Transmission pieces 21

   Dagger 23

   Forces of nature 23

   Black Hole 24

Synchronization 25

Rapport 26

How to Practice 28

Conclusion 29

   Other books by Jack N. Raven Publishing

Introduction

They say the eyes are the windows to the soul. What they'll see on the other side of that window is what well specifically use to manufacture the desired effects on them!

In this book we shall be exploring the many different ways we can use the power of eye contact to get what we want. For the vast majority, this channel of communication is underutilized-even nonexistent. There are so many nifty things we can do with this technology that will allow us to be more attractive, persuasive and overall more powerful! It will help you create the "it" factor, that makes you so damn convincing, they can't quite put a finger on how you're actually doing it!

There is a section below called "Mission Impossible Seductions" which teaches how to use eye contact to seduce a target in front of the boyfriend. From there you can apply the same technology in other fields where covert tactics are needed.

In the last section of this book will be the "raw ingredients" to eye contact subcommunications that will allow you to create powerful transmissions for higher success. That is just the tip of the iceberg. That should get your creative juices flowing on how to create an infinite numbers of flavors and subtle adjustments to create ANY emotional and psychological effect you want on anyone!

Specifics

Specifically, the whites of the eye allow the canvas to be used for communication—but that is not all. The size of the eye will also communicate interest or disinterest by the way it enlarges or widens. How the eyes squint are also indications of emotions—but it has to be taken in the proper context with other verbal and nonverbal communications that are taking place. The eyebrows, if drawn close together, may communicate anger, surprise, attention, interest, or even disinterest. The focus of the eyes determine if a person is interested or is glazing onwards into being bored to death.

The intensity of eye contact determines the intensity of interest. Do your eyes just happen to land in that particular location? Or visit laser-focused attention looking at that spot.

Humans, compared to the 220 species of primates who have no whites in their eyes at all, have eyeballs that are meant to communicate. Our irises and pupils float on this white canvas, allowing the other individual to lead us. This is meant, by design, as a form of nonverbal communication. Other species with no observable whites in their eyes are not designed to be used for communication.

Those whites allow others to see exactly what you're looking at, and what we are even thinking almost. Anthropologists believe that human eyes evolve in order to learn cooperation and better collect with other humans. This is extremely valuable in building civilization. Our eyes are not just designed for looking or perceiving the world. It's actually designed as a tool of communication with others.

Duration of Gaze
How long you have been looking at something determines interest or disinterest. The less you look obviously means you're not that interested. Unless you are deliberately trying to be coy, which happens when you are absolutely interested in those pairs of knockers, but you can't look too long for obvious reasons

Strong eye contact
Having a strong neutral eye contact by itself already makes you more powerful than someone with avoidant gaze. This is going to be the baseline for any of the other techniques in this book. Though not all require strong or high intensity eye work? We need that extra bandwidth. It's better to have the range and tone it down, than be in need of that extra power later on, realizing you lack the strength of gaze.

I'll give you 3 exercises you can practice right now.

1. If you're not used to looking at people's eyes? Practice on animals like your dog or cat. Try not to blink and keep at it as long as possible. Along with duration of gaze, make sure to practice that deep and penetrating gaze! It should be penetrating like ice pick! Practice as often as you can and when you're ready try to practice on people. You can

be intense without looking hostile, by smizing (smiling with your eyes) and sending good, positive energies.

2. Pick a spot on the wall and look at it intently, also trying to ice pick into it with your eyes. Try to hold it as long as possible with blinking. The next higher level of practice from this is looking at a bright spot as long as possible also without blinking.

3. Not just for developing strong eye contact, but the rest of the exercises in this book. Turn on the TV and eye-project strong on their eyes!

Other ways to practice to increase your eye game is on the last chapter of this book.

Eye contact in job hunting

Employers like candidates with strong eye contact because of what it says about the character of the potential applicant. Having strong, powerful and deliberate eye contact is one indicator of a person's confidence. Especially in jobs requiring confidence and self determination- it's one of the things the HR personnel look for in their people. Applicants that can subcommunicate true confidence are crucial especially in sales positions where you are tasked to talk to high-level shakers and movers like CEOs and other high ranking clientele. You can't make your clients feel confident about your widget, if you're not confident yourself! If a salesperson can't look at a prospect in the eyes, what do you think it subcommunicates? Lack of confidence in the product or service maybe because it's inferior?

It's a confidence that penetrates the target. You're not looking at the superficial body but are penetrating through: almost trying to control and fully read what's there!

You're not really looking at the person, you are subcommunicating that you are an equal that commands equal respect! It's how you look at the individual in that deeply piercing way, shattering the bullshit and faux facades!

If that is not possible because you're too intimidated or scared? You can cheat this by not directly looking at that person's eyes, just looking at the tip of his nose or his brows.

Rewards and Punishments through the eyes

Classical conditioning is about capturing behaviors and either rewarding it to promote the repetition of that behavior or catching negative behaviors, punishing accordingly to discourage that behavior. This does not have to be a conscious process. People even animals learn naturally whenever you associate desired behaviors to rewards and behaviors we want to discourage with punishments. This has been automatically happening and that's how people even animals get trained deliberately or accidentally.

Rewarding

It is anything that either feels good to the individual or

strokes her ego etc.
How do you do that? When you catch a good thing she just did? Proactively act on it for example by showing your appreciation, by making a more committed eye contact and even using your entire body to reinforce the message.

Sub-communicate that you are impressed—that you think she's intelligent, beautiful, and that you think she's talented in whatever it is she does. You can sub-communicate all of this through your eyes. On the most basic level, recognize the person's existence. Just by looking at her and letting her know that she's there is already a reward in itself.

Coming back to rewards, another way could be by widening your eyes to sub-communicate that you are becoming fascinated more and more either by her, what she is saying, or both.
More mechanical ways could be squinting at her or flirting through the eyes, etc.

Punishments

Do the exact opposite of what I said in the previous section. You can show the opposite of fascination, which is showing signs of boredom. You can roll your eyes or create the expression that you are about to fall asleep. You could also look fierce or hostile towards her. You can just antagonize her with looks alone. You can even look at her head to toe, and many other things—just use your imagination.

By pretending the person doesn't exist, like how we see vagabonds and peddlers on the street-we invalidate their existence!

The eye communications to punish should not be accidental. The person has to FEEL your message.

Indicators of Interest

Indicators of interest (or IOI's) are used in the seduction community to determine whether a target is showing signs of attraction, or that you need more work to get her attracted. The most obvious signals could be that she's looking at you like you are the most interesting person there. She's looking at your chest; she gives you that puppy-dog look that she's almost mesmerized by you. When you're talking, 100 percent of her attention is on you!

There are some not so obvious signals that may require a little bit of decoding. Both indicators of interest, and opposite, which is "IOD", or indicators of disinterests are all important to read. We'll get to that in a little bit.

Using the same metrics from earlier, you can tell a lot by the direction she's looking at, the intensity, and many other things. Women are actually better at this—sending and receiving nonverbal communications. The average guy has no idea what's going on—we have to be taught these skills.

These things come naturally for women, they are

hardwired to be sensitive to these invisible messages because they are keenly aware of this channel of communication, you can now use this to send out the desired messages. If you're going to use this to flirt, the same indicators of interest and disinterest can be calibrated accordingly to send the appropriate message that you want. As she is talking, if you want to sub-communicate that you actually appreciate her more than for her looks, instead of looking at her boobs or ass, you can just be looking at her face where her eyes are!

If she just bought this bracelet and you just noticed her eyes looking at it trying to direct attention to it? She would appreciate it if you would pay attention to the bracelet and how great it looks on her!

A woman just gives out signals on the things that she wants to be appreciated for, and you can use your eyes along with your words to compliment. Some women from time to time need their ego stroked. You can easily do this with no effort just by looking at their faces and appreciating their beauty. A woman just likes to be thought of as beautiful; even those who get looked a lot. They can still appreciate that nonverbal compliment of just being stared at, and nonverbally told how gorgeous they are.

You can appreciate <u>non-physical</u> traits through your eyes. For example, if she sings well, she might think, "Are your eyes showing appreciation?" Well, you can just mentally focus and sub-communicate that you are appreciating the music and look like you are mesmerized by her voice.

You can look at any one specific thing exactly, but overall, it can easily be communicated, and she'll fully get it! Understand how subtexts work and all this becomes a piece of cake!

If the target is a chef, how would you compliment her cooking with only your eyes? Simple! Look at the food she's prepared, and how a five-year-old fat kid looks at an ice cream truck! Like he can't wait to eat it. Almost like it's the most beautiful thing he's ever seen in his entire life! Then, when you actually put it in your mouth, you are intoxicated, like you are in heaven or something. If you're there during the preparation, you can also show appreciation by how impressed you are how meticulous, professional and talented she is.

No words needed to be spoken at all.

The problem with over-complimenting is that you could come off weak, trying to impress her: being a kiss-ass! You don't have be that transparent. Compliments can be relayed without words!

How to show fascination with the eyes

By the same principles of subtext again, you can just look into her eyes and mentally go through a list of the things you appreciate about her. It does not have to be real because you can use anything real or imagined. Let this be real in your mind—whether made up or not—like you have to be going soon, as you're looking at her! For example, you can say in your mind how you like her for being that one in a million chick or that she's smart (even if she's not) or that she is a good dancer or whatever it is that you truly like. Make believe that she has it and appreciate it one by one as you're looking into her eyes. Make believe that these traits belong to her! She will just get that message somehow. She'll understand it and receive it as a compliment although you haven't said anything! It doesn't lower your value at all.

Eye communications for instant isolation

When you get the target engaged and when you're looking eye to eye lost in each other's gazes, it's like the world disappears and only you and this person exists. That is kind of effect we want! To isolate or be with the target with you in private without moving anywhere! Mentally once a target is engaged completely it generates the same effect, though in reality she hasn't moved.

The more common way to isolate is physically move a target away from her friends. That's still necessary for some many isolation needs, but in other situations we only need to immerse and get the target engaged by creating that virtual couples bubble that only the two of you live in.

To do this, there must be a reason why both you are looking at each other intently in that way. It normally happens in normal interactions between people talking about a topic that deeply engages them.

So one way to go about this is to come up with highly engaging material or topic, they have no choice but to be fully immersed in the experience in this moment!

You can do so much and say so much with your eyes alone! Knowing the technology you can also transmit the same verbally and nonverbally with your other senses.

Occasionally the friends might be alarmed by the level of engagement of their friend. So they try to run confusion by breaking her state. Once the state interrupt happens, and you haven't done enough work? That may be the end of it! State interrupt happens when you are in a state of trance that you're mesmerized and deeply entrained so the friend(s) try to interrupt that deep engagement by changing topics, pulling her away to dance, asking a dumb question etc.

Making subtexts real

How do you make subtext real? You make it real to the observers by first making it feel real inside of you! You have to feel the sensations, actually see and hear the experiences on the inside for others to be convinced. You can make that special look that you've met someone before, and this accidental meeting is actually the second meeting. She will get it! She might actually be persuaded to believe that you've met before, even though you really haven't. This works because it is open-ended as long as she can be 100 percent sure you haven't met, and that there is a possibility that you have.

This is so accurate that those doing surveillance on targets, even if they are using or wearing misleading uniforms, they can tell ranks, just based on the eye contact. Who's calling the shots, and who is following. Though they may try to play the role of being the inferior, eye contact alone can determine who is who in the pecking order.

You cannot convince others if you are not convinced yourself. Not only must you be convinced, you must be absolutely flawless in your beliefs. There must not be any holes because you use the indomitable belief to out-frame the other person.

Any hesitations or insecurities? Expect other people to sense it! Make it strong and unbreakable? It can shatter the foundation of their beliefs!

Be a hundred percent absolutely sure whether it is real or not is irrelevant. You just have to believe it as if it were real!

That was just an example of the many things you can do with this ability. Just copy how people look at different people or the relationships in their lives. A subordinate looks at her boss differently from how she would look at a peer, close friend, a lover, etc. There are patterns that you need to observe closely, then list them down and get the exact physicality (how something looks physically). Once you do this, you can copy them exactly and generate great results-maybe even identical results if you do it properly.

The Intimidation Look

Eye contact by forceful dominance. The main objective here is to make them comply through coercion again all done through the eyes! The fear will push them along in full compliance if your frame and gaze is dominant enough. Again, nothing has to be communicated verbally—this is all done through the eyes. You can do this through subtext.

We can also adjust, making it stronger or weaker. Particularly, if we just met this person or haven't even been formally introduced you may tone this down.

The underlying subtext when you're trying to intimidate through your eyes is forceful-dominance, and that they must absolutely comply. Then, they must stand down or be prepared to face the consequences. The subtext is, "you better do what I tell you to do, or else I'll slit your throat! I am the one and only person who has an opinion here, and what you think is irrelevant. You don't have to like me, you don't have to agree with what I say, and you just have to obey my wishes!"

You can practice this and other looks by involving the physicality of how your entire body, gestures would move to kill an insect etc. As you get used to the energy or message plus the aid of physically expressing it through your gestures, punching on the bag etc, you can remove the physical movements, and all that remains are the eyes.

There is a layer of the toned-down variation of this—it's the parent's 'all commanding' look. It's what a parent would structure to her children to make them comply. It's almost the same, except there is no slit-your-throat part. "You must do as I say, because I am your parent!" The kind of intimidation that you broadcast when you do this is not hostile, just authoritative and commanding. The other one is more hostile and demanding, in the sense that you will suffer dire consequences if you do not comply. The type from the first section is of higher status and more dominant.

If you look down, or look away, this denotes lower status. It shows subservience. In certain cultures, you're not even allowed to look at another's eyes because it is a sign of disrespect. You're only allowed to look at them from the neck down. Only someone of equal or higher stature can look them in the eye. Conversely, one who isn't looking deep in the eyes is showing signs of intimidation. They are therefore of lower status, based on eye communications. Sometimes, this may even be misconstrued as trying to hide something or being guilty.

Forcing submission in a Seduction setting

Women find it sexy when they can be dominated. This happens if your frame is stronger than hers and your energy and body language is not backing out in any way. You're actually doing the opposite—you're forcing your dominance onto the target, but not too much that it becomes too intimidating. Just enough that you generate the submission effect. The more you polarize to your masculinity, it will move and polarize her femininity, and that is the correct order of things between men and women.

Dweebs who are weaker, makes the women dominate can't cause gut level attraction. That is not the right order of things. The rightful place of men by nature is that the female's femininity should be by the side, or under the male's dominant energy. By successfully dominating through your stronger frame and eye contact, you're generating that gut level attraction they can't explain but desire!

In order to show strength, your gaze has to be solid. Not referring to just the physically of a gaze—also what's powering it underneath. Don't think of controlling just the physical, think of actually controlling the energy behind the gaze, making it naturally as deliciously solid and forcefully dominant as possible.

Even the tiniest shift in energy can be felt by a sensitive target—especially women. The slightest faltering and micro gestures can be seen and observed. That ever so slight backing out in body language and energy can reveal your betaness or weakness. Don't think of faking this stuff, your inner-game should be solid, so work on it from a position of authenticity!

If you can create that solid alpha dominant energy from within, it naturally comes out when you seek submission and dominance from the targets. It's all a matter of calibration if you want to polarize a female target, or if you want to be more forceful and use it for hostile intimidation. Calibrate intensity and energy differences.

Mission Impossible Seductions

Mission impossible seductions require the utmost discretion and secrecy. These are situations, forbidden situations, or seductions that you're not supposed to engage in. For example, you can't hit on a friend's girlfriend or wife. You can't hit on someone who you work with—stuff like that. For that, you need covert means of generating the necessary emotions, and internal experiences of the target without being exposed as to your true intentions. There are many ways to seduce covertly, but someone with a trained eye, experience, and is good in the game, can easily detect this a mile away! Try as you may, but your ruse will get exposed eventually even through the use of the best covert tactics—verbally, or nonverbally. Don't even think about using standard seduction techniques because that would get you easily exposed and caught! Well, unless you're dealing with untrained targets and observers, you may get away.

For this level of game, your best weapon is eye seduction. You must be able to generate and sub-communicate the proper feelings, emotions, and concepts in the right order—in order, to generate the effects that you want to without being seen by the people surrounding the target. Someone who understands this stuff, let's say an expert level PUA (Pick up Artist), can see the eye game too, so be careful.

However, because of the angles, the narrow angles, if you tilt it just the right way so only the target can see your eye communications, then the people around her will hardly see it. They might be able to catch part of it, but not get the transmission in its entirety! Women are exceptionally sharp at this and even they won't be able to catch it if you play with the angles and anticipate being observed. Women are highly responsive to mirror neurons—meaning they don't have to see, hear, or use it to their physical senses to actually feel emotion. They for certain are sure that you are up to something, but unless there is actual proof or they actually see the moves, then there is no plausible deniability to your actions.

There are no actual incriminating actions and all they're relying on are the mirror neurons—a woman's intuition, gut level instincts in general—then they've got nothing!

Besides, you have at your disposal tools to throw them off your scent and to conceal your intentions. As long as you have ready-made explanations for every action you make, they won't be able to pin it on you. Now, this is an extremely high-level game—we're talking about a hard target surrounded by educated and experienced seducers and operators—this is not just the civilian grade, run-of-the-mill, average Joe trying to seduce the average game. So, this is the worst-case scenario and you may not need to go that far ordinarily.

Knowing eye seductions you can move safely, covertly and effectively.

Transmission pieces

These are individual pieces that you can use as delivery vehicles for your messages. You can use them to layer your ring of sub-communications. The key to robust sub-communication is subtext, and layering that subtext in depth. The more you can sculpt it and add as many pieces—the right pieces—and exactly the right mixture of recipes, the more effective and well rounded it becomes. Nothing should be accidental. Everything you do should be intentional just like each and every micro-gesture and expression, intonation, and nonverbals of the best actors in the world. They are never accidental—they are always precise. Their bodies are precise instruments channeling these layers of sub-communication to express the message through various other channels with their eyes, touch, words, and matching intonations—even their costumes, props, and whatever it is that they are using in their environment.

Even on their bodies as well, and inside their heads, are all deliberate pieces meant for a specific set of effects. The mark of a professional is sophistication and intention. Nothing is ever accidental, and those that are accidental? It's there by design! You should include seemingly random or soft pieces to minimize the sharpness or the appearance of professionalism to generate the correct effect and minimize the target's resistance. After all who likes to be sold to? Who likes to be gamed or manipulated?

Another way to put this is that some may get intimidated or become paranoid if you appear too polished! Like, if you're an actor playing the role of a beggar, and you look too cliché for the part? Too scripted and polished might not be that convincing just because it's too textbook!

But even the dirt is precisely put in place for a specific psychological affect. Think of a tank or bulldozer for this quality and it is useful for messages that you want to obliterate resistance and out frame them by force! For purposes of intimidation, for example, we're trying to force submission to break resistance—especially your real message, whatever it may be, will have more power if you can layer it or have it injected in the bulldozer metaphor. It will destroy everything in its path, completely indomitable, invulnerable—and similar mental visuals. You have to be able to imagine or visualize what they're thinking and your tank can obliterate it! There could be some explosions involved or it could shatter into thousands of pieces—whatever case it may be—the sense of weight, strength, and forceful energy of the tank!

Dagger

This is more of a tool for penetration as opposed to obliteration from the tank metaphor. For example, there is an object right in front of you—the dagger stabs and penetrates at the core without destroying—it will scratch but will not destroy the entire object. It just stabs though; it doesn't need to destroy-just deep penetration. Just like how you would stab a slice of meat with an ice-pick. It just goes in and comes right back out—nothing is destroyed, tissues still intact.

Forces of nature

You can visualize this as any force of nature—such as typhoons, tsunamis etc. But this is more of an abstract concept or a delivery vehicle to empower your transmission. Force of nature means nothing can stop you, because you are a force of nature! What happens when an immovable object meets unstoppable force? For example, you are trying to inject the idea that she is into you, which is using your willpower to overpower hers. She is immovable but your will is unstoppable. What happens? Nothing happens because both are forces of nature! That's actually a trick question. Coincidentally, both are useful resources and the immovable object is also another concept that can be useful to create stability, immovable grounding of your without being imposing like tsunamis, tank and other concepts or energies that overrun their frames or resistances!

The force of nature invalidates anything outside your message. It's sort of like, "It doesn't matter what you think, what I think prevails because I am a force of nature! We can try to pretend your opinion has weight but ultimately what you believe and thing is irrelevant. You're just you, and I'm the force of nature. No contest. There's only just one outcome when you battle any force of nature…defeat.

Immovable force is easier to imagine when it is dynamic. A dynamic version, as was mentioned previously, is the unstoppable force of nature (like a tsunami).

Unstoppable force that is dormant, unmoving, deeply rooted like a rock, it's sitting in one place is the immovable force of nature. NOTHING can move it! It's beyond manipulation!

Black Hole

Black holes are vortices that have intense, irresistible gravities literally everything including light, sound, time get sucked into it! This is also another force of nature so powerful that they really have no choice but to be sucked into it.

The point with concept is to imagine the gravity- irresistible gravity. This works for messages or transmissions like: In a seduction application when trying to flip the script and swap gender roles. If you're a man and you want to be the woman being chased? Consider that for a second. The person being chased creates an immense level of attraction that women can't resist hitting on him!

In terms of general charisma, you are not really doing anything but you are so magnetic, people are drawn to you naturally!

In that sense this is the opposite of the tank and tsunami—which are male or positive energies—trying to force on some energy. This is easier to see with actresses trying to play coy, and trying to make the male characters chase after them. It's all about creating gravity.

In a physical sense, a woman, a gorgeous woman, walks into a bar, makes brief eye contact with any man, and the man sees it. When the man reciprocates or shows sexual interest? The girl pulls back. It's that pullback action that generates the gravity.

Synchronization

This pattern is about being wherever she is emotionally and mentally. It's about being in synch. Imagine you're both jet-fighter pilots—you're trying to match what she's doing exactly to the millimeter. She tries to lose you, you maneuver to match her. If she dives, you dive. Your objective is to synchronize to her by whatever means. If she is feeling the excitement and emotion of excitement, you have to see where the target is and what she's feeling and try to be there with her!

This works in reverse as well and naturally happens when people are developing deep rapport. You go this way; they naturally follow without anyone really doing it consciously! This is called pacing, leading, and mirroring. Why let that happen naturally, when you can initiate the process yourself? Whatever it is, you're trying to create on the targets mind through your eye contact and projection it has to have that specific intention—a deliberate desire to either synch up or make her synch up to you! The difference that makes all the difference is the intention! Don't just do this mechanically, but actually want to synch up!

Rapport

You blink approximately at the same time. She is either breathing, or blinking her eyes while speaking. You can even base off the pacing from her heartbeat if you can hear it. Anything that has a rhythm can be used to mirror, pace and build deep rapport. And you can do that by your blink rate and other eye communications.

Comedy improvisation is about "yes-ing". Anything the participants contribute, you build the fire on the last offering. You also do the same to build rapport by "yes-ing", and being the same nonverbally. Here is an example:

When she says she likes dogs or likes to eat pizza, you can show agreement through your eyes by showing interest and desire. You can also nod your head. Those are forms of agreement that build rapport that show her you're on the same page. You can also show disagreement to things that she finds disagreeable.

It's not always advisable to always be agreeing to what the other person is saying because it makes you look like a pushover and weak! The added benefit of nonverbal rapport building is that you can verbally disagree so that she doesn't think you're weak while agreeing non-verbally. You get the benefit of both because you are agreeing while disagreeing. When you do this sort of nonverbal communication, you want to primarily talk to the subconscious mind. Whenever you verbal disagreements you're talking to the conscious mind. It will register that you disagreed, yet a part of her recognizes that you are actually on the same page because you are agreeing only through your eyes and body language.

Another trick to eye subcommunications is that whatever she said, assume you said first! She is merely trying to agree with it. In other words, she, not you is doing the effort of rapport building. Although in reality we are the ones trying to build rapport with her? It's a mindfuck, through our <u>assumptive</u> sub communications, force framing and gestures that she, not us is trying to build rapport!

All these things can be communicated just by your eyes, but can be supplemented by words and your other body parts for increased effect.

How to Practice

This is most important, and without this, you just won't achieve any results!

You can practice this on actual targets (whoever you consider to be the targets of your eye communications), or you can use VP (Virtual Practice from my other book), or just practice on the mirror and anyone with an eyeball (lol).

Using VP, you can play movies etc, and be that character and try to persuade the other characters you're interacting with virtually. You can drastically save time too by operating in fast time! For more details please check out "The Art of Virtual Practice 2"

For standard training, you can just PROJECT that message to try to MANIPULATE the other person into doing something, thinking of something or feeling it!

As it were imagine you had telekinesis, willfully trying to move an object from across the room. It feels like that! The opposite of that is just passively visualizing something which is weaker than actually, trying to forcefully commanding them!

Passive visualizations, has its place too, but for the most part the other one is stronger. Passive is needed when a target feels your overbearing energy for example. You just need to give him more space and tone down your energy projections.

Conclusion

Congratulations! You now have at your disposal tools, powerful tools kept by the Pros to make you exceptionally persuasive in your chosen field of endeavor! You can be more intimidating, dominant, powerful, seductive, respectable-whatever it is you desire, you can now create just with your eyes!

I must warn you however this requires practice. You must create a specific message then keep on practicing that until you no longer have to think about it! It happens on autopilot-unconscious competence!

That is important because we are always juggling things all at once. No special effort is needed to communicate through the eyes. We must reach that stage this becomes second nature like breathing!

Being in the seduction field, I personally have a stash of different recipes designed to elicit specific effects. I have eye communication recipes that when I look at someone, it's like I've been having sex with her for months! Or that were soul mates, or that I'm her boss and many others. Each one had to be practiced separately that all I need to do is will it and everything just happens automatically!

Please don't underestimate the power of being in rapport and in synch with the target. It makes any communication and persuasion far more powerful than without it (rapport). Though you can achieve reasonable success without working on rapport directly? It's better if you have it. Persuasion without rapport building requires a stronger frame or flawless belief in your message/transmission that the targets naturally buy into yours! If you've ever just wanted to surrender to the reality or vision of a powerful politician, salesman, ceo etc, that's how it looks and feels like in the field.

Trust in the process. Trust in the technology. This stuff works! All you need to do is watch models and actors who have their own variations of these techniques.

This guide is not intended as and may not be construed as an alternative to or a substitute for professional mental counseling, therapy or medical services and advice.

The authors, publishers, and distributors of this guide have made every effort to ensure the validity, accuracy, and timely nature of the information presented here. However, no guarantee is made, neither direct nor implied, that the information in this guide or the techniques described herein are suitable for or applicable to any given individual person or group of persons, nor that any specific result will be achieved. The authors, publishers, and distributors of this guide will be held harmless and without fault in all situations and causes arising from the use of this information by any person, with or without professional medical supervision. The information contained in this book is for informational and entertainment purposes only. It not intended as a professional advice or a recommendation to act.

No part of this book may be reproduced or transmitted in any form whatsoever, electronic, or mechanical, including photocopying, recording, or by any informational storage or retrieval system without express permission from the author.

© Copyright 2013, Jack N. Raven
Date of publication January 15, 2014
All rights reserved.

ABOUT THE AUTHOR

Jack N. Raven finished AB Legal Management and MBA-Management. He has studied many areas of applied Psychology, Manipulation and Persuasion such as Hypnosis, Neuro-Linguistic Programming (equivalent Practitioner and Master Practitioner training level), Tradecraft, Sales, Marketing, Copywriting, Seduction (Practically having studied and experienced and gotten success with beautiful women in all major systems available i.e. Natural, Indirect, Direct, SS systems etc; Sedona Method ™, Emotional Freedom Techniques™. He has over a decade of experience and training in esoteric systems like Qi-Gong, Bardon Hermetics, Keylontic Sciences, Quantum Touch ™ and other energy healing systems.

He has studied various martial arts and miscellaneous self improvement systems and technologies.

His current passion is Digital Arts and Fashion Photography.

If you have any questions please LIKE and PM me at my facebook.

http://www.facebook.com/jacknraven

Other books by Jack N. Raven Publishing

The Seduction Force Multiplier 1- Bring Out Your FULL Seduction powers through
the Power of Routines, Drills, Scripting and Protocols

This is book #1 and a must read if you are serious in exploring and maximizing your seduction potential. Includes more in depth information on how to construct, internalize and the advantages of Scripting versus Natural game convos.

The Seduction Force Multiplier 2 - Scripts and Routines Book

This is the main routines manual which contains the full lines and routines, that are shortened in this book. More than 700 of them!

Also includes the full audio of the routines you can listen to.

The Seduction Force Multiplier 3- PUA Routines Memory Transplant Package

This is book #3 that includes nearly 2 hours of audio. A one of a kind system that allows you to easily memorize about 700 routines and lines from book #2, in just days!

Imagine the dramatic improvements in your game, if you can internalize hundreds of routines! Routines you wont have a problem summoning. All on muscle memory, reflexive, ready to go, just automatically flows out of your mouth without effort in the field!

The Seduction Force Multiplier 4 - Situational PUA Scripts and Routines

In this book, specific routines or scripts have been made focusing on the most common scenarios facing the PUAs.

These are specific game recipes exactly made covering that particular environment or situation! From opening to mid-game, everything is handed to you.

The Seduction Force Multiplier V - Target Auto Response Package

This book covers over 160 target/set reactions so you wont have to rack your brains coming up with responses, and so you can handle each reaction effectively!

Over 900 lines covering 160 reactions so you won't have to rack your brains coming up with effective responses.
Also includes methods to INTERNALIZE/MEMORIZE the material.

The Seduction Force Multiplier VI - PUA Innergame, Mindsets and Attitudes

THis book contains the helpful mindsets proven succesful by thousands of PUAs, veteran and rookies. These are the missing pieces to an already powerful outergame repertoire.
Also contained in the book: how to game JEDI, or nonverbally, allowing you to be whoever you want to be!

Not only in terms of improving your seduction powers, it will also help you become not only solid on the outside, but rock solid from within!

Shielded Heart - How To Stop Yourself From Falling For A Seduction Target

For one reason or another you probably don't want to fall in love for that girl or guy. This book is the only book of its kind dealing with this sensitive subject! This will make you invulnerable to strong feelings, in order for you to not fall for a seduction target.

How To Cheat Proof Your Relationships

A thought provoking book, entirely about the subject of seducing someone in a relationship! Either as the aggressor/Player, or the lover wanting to protect his or her love from being seduced by 3rd party Operators and Seducers.

Secrets to Hacking Your Brain- Be Your Own Therapist

A book on the best techniques from various self help disciplines like NLP, Hypnosis, EFT etc, on how to remove any feelings, and emotions at will!

Hypno Machines - How To Convert Every Object In Your Environment As a Device For Psychological and Emotional Manipulator

Based on the NLP principle of Anchoring, this book will allow you to convert literally everything that exists in the world, as your change agents, that work automatically in the background creating emotional and psychological developments and changes.

The same concept can be used in persuasion too, if you are inclined.

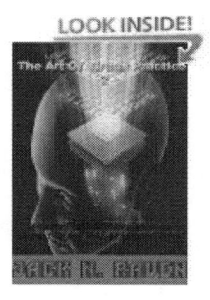

The Art Of Virtual Practice 2 - Learning and Mastery Of Any Skill At Lighting Speeds!

It takes about 10,000 hours to be a MASTER at any craft. By following the techniques on this book? You can cut that that to a fraction of the time!

You can get more field time/practice time by doing these special techniques-anytime, anywhere! Imagine any skill, you can learn to master it at a fraction of the time!

How to Operate with Your Full Potential and Talents

If you've always wanted to perform at your 100% best but couldn't? Then this is for you!

By figuring out your deepest motivations and "why"s, every part of what you're doing becomes more charged, solid, and FORCEFUL!

You will feel energized, centered, and fully aligned with your full powers, talents and capabilities! Alignment is the key to unlocking your full potential!

How To Master Resilience And Be Invincible To Life's Disappointments And Failures

By developing the proper mindsets, and seeing what these negative, hurtful energies for what they truly are? The reader can strengthen his fortitude, and almost enjoy failures, as a means of reaching the higher levels!

And no, this book won't tell you to live in a fairy tale world, and stay positive all the time!

The X-Factor Manual - Learn How To be A Model Even If You Don't Look Like One

A book for increasing sex appeal, though written with models in mind? The principles and techniques also apply to regular men and women, who want to increase attractiveness using modeling techniques, as well as techniques from other disciplines.

The Age Erase System - Hypnotic Anti Aging Serum

You don't have to settle with getting old. Just with the power of your mind, you can reverse the ravaging effects of time on your health, organs, skin and even looks!

Try this for a month, and tell me it doesn't work! I dare you!

Develop Insane Self Confidence and Naturally Unleash The Supermodel Within

This program will allow you to unleash the hidden gorgeous creature hiding inside of you. This program will easily unleash, in no time at all, your sexy self confidence and sex appeal.
Field tested to give you absolute results!

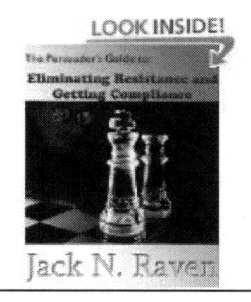

The Persuaders Guide To Eliminating Resistance And Getting Compliance

If you are a Persuader (who isn't), this book can teach you how to navigate and make your offers to minimize, even eliminate resistance from subjects/targets!

If you can master resistance? You can master persuasion!

The Art of Invisible Compliance - How To Make People Do What You Want Effortlessly

This book includes the Ins and Outs of making people do what you want, as covertly or overtly as you want.
If you've wondered how Intelligence Operatives make people do things short of coercion, this is how they do it.

The principles work in any persuasion setting, whether seduction, sales, marketing, anything that involves getting a desired action(compliance) from people. This book will teach you how to move INVISIBLY to get what you want, without revealing your position yourself! Very useful for covert persuasions.

Unstoppable and Fearless - Know What You Want and Get It

By knowing what you want, you now need the courage to actually get it and win! This book explores and gives you practical steps how you can reduce the fears, and make you unusually comfortable with fears and places outside your comfort zones.

Just Go- Having The Courage and Will to Pursue Your Dreams

Most people are afraid to go after what they want, let alone actually pursue it! This book will help to set you on your way!

How To Make Better Life Decisions

This book will help you to make crucial life decisions in every facet of life!

It helps give you the tools and elements to consider in weighing the many possible courses of actions and alternatives, to help you choose the absolute best decisions each and every time!

How To Diet Like a Machine- Make Any Diet Program Work With Ease

This book will give you the tools to PERMANENTLY brainwash yourself to loving the new diet meal program. You'll hate it in the beginning, but you'll grow to love it!
Because everyone hates diets, and the only way a sane person will want to keep it, is if gets reprogrammed forcefully!

Friends into Lovers: Escape and Never be Trapped In The Friendzone Ever Again!

If you're currently trapped or would like to be un-trapped in this dreaded zone now and in the future? You absolutely must check out the information in this book. Some people are born almost to be forever categorized in this zone, while others just seem to have "it", they can't get friendzoned if they wanted! This book will show you how to solve this problem-PERMANENTLY!

The Permanent Anti-jealousy Solution

This ugly poison of an emotion destroys relationships, be constantly hurt by cold-hearted players, even destroy self-esteem! Just what is "jealousy" and how do we make it disappear?

By the end of reading this book, you'll be leaving with specific tools to achieve exactly that! By understanding what is jealousy, you'll be protected against its ill effects while having the power to create this effect on targets! You'll also catch a glimpse how we get victimized using this powerful emotion.

The TEN Game Operations Manual: How To Get Extremely Gorgeous 10s Consistently and Predictably!

Most Seduction Gurus and systems ignore the existence of 10 game. Most PUAs or Seducers will never get 10s until the end of their seduction careers because seduction systems are designed for regular girls! The 10s require specialized game, without knowing these secrets? Be part of the statistics!

How Not To Give a Shit!: The Art of Not Caring

Would you like to learn how to stop giving a damn? There are situations where you just need to remove emotional attachments to people and situations to function properly.

In this book we go into great detail on the forces why we care (when this is not a luxury), and how we can dismantle these elements effectively! To liberate ourselves from caring too much, stop caring what others think-to make us emotionally detached!

Perfecting Your Game: How To Reach Mastery Through Perfection Of Game!

This book is all about improving your performance in your chosen industry/game/craft/sport and reaching master class as quickly as humanly possible! It contains ideas where to get more tools, more powers to enhance your performance and maximize the performance you're getting from the existing ones, without having to add anything new.

Manipulative Eye Contact Techniques: Install thoughts and feelings just with your eyes!

This book will teach you powerful, easy, and covert techniques that will give you the power to "suggest" or install any thought, picture, feelings to any target, any time!

Made in United States
Orlando, FL
04 August 2024